A Crabtree Branches Book

Let's Go Fish

DEEP SEA FISHING

By Kerri Mazzarella

CRABTREE
Publishing Company
www.crabtreebooks.com

T0020246

School-to-Home Support for Caregivers and Teachers

This high-interest book is designed to motivate striving students with engaging topics while building fluency, vocabulary, and an interest in reading. Here are a few questions and activities to help the reader build upon his or her comprehension skills.

Before Reading:

- *What do I think this book is about?*
- *What do I know about this topic?*
- *What do I want to learn about this topic?*
- *Why am I reading this book?*

During Reading:

- *I wonder why...*
- *I'm curious to know...*
- *How is this like something I already know?*
- *What have I learned so far?*

After Reading:

- *What was the author trying to teach me?*
- *What are some details?*
- *How did the photographs and captions help me understand more?*
- *Read the book again and look for the vocabulary words.*
- *What questions do I still have?*

Extension Activities:

- *What was your favorite part of the book? Write a paragraph on it.*
- *Draw a picture of your favorite thing you learned from the book.*

TABLE OF CONTENTS

WHERE TO FISH

Deep sea fishing is practiced all over the world. It can be done as a sport or as a job. It is one of the most exciting types of fishing.

It is sometimes called "big game fishing" or "sport fishing." It takes place offshore in the ocean. This type of fishing requires a boat.

Deep sea fishing requires more than just a hook and line. You will need many styles of fishing poles and bait.

Most coastal towns in the U.S. offer sport fishing trips. These are also known as a **fishing charter**. This is a fun activity to try while on vacation.

FUN FACTS

Venice, Louisiana, is home to some of the best sport fishing in the world.

TYPES OF FISH

The biggest fish are caught while deep sea fishing. Many anglers enjoy the fight of reeling in a huge fish. It can sometimes take hours for a fish to be brought to the boat.

black marlin

blue marlin

white marlin

Marlin and **sailfish** are normally released. Marlin can grow up to 12 feet (3.7 m) and weigh up to 2,000 pounds (907 kg)!

FUN FACTS

Sailfish are smaller than marlin. The record sailfish was caught off the coast of Ecuador in 1947. It weighed 221 pounds (100 kg).

Some other exciting sport fish are **tuna**, swordfish, wahoo, amberjack, snapper, grouper, and the beautiful dolphin. Not the porpoise kind!

tuna

These fish are all considered great to eat.

mahi mahi

FUN FACTS
Other names for the dolphin fish are mahi mahi and dorado. Mahi mahi have beautiful colors.

SAFETY AND RULES

Deep sea fishing requires preparation. You will be fishing from a boat several miles from shore. It is important to use caution and stay safe. Always listen to the boat captain.

The boat should have electronics for navigation, an **anchor**, and rope. It should also have a first aid kit.

FUN FACTS

Boats are required to have special safety kits and life jackets.

Deep sea fishing can be exciting and fast-paced, especially when there is a fish on the line. Be aware of your surroundings to avoid getting injured. It is important to bring plenty of food and water.

You will need to purchase a saltwater fishing license and be aware of the fishing regulations for the area you are planning to fish.

Many people get sea sick from the rocking of the boat.

FUN FACTS

You will likely be out on the water for several hours. Sunscreen and a hat should be worn to avoid getting sunburned.

RODS AND TACKLE

FUN FACTS

The good thing about a fishing charter is that everything you need will be provided.

There are many deep sea fishing rods, reels, and **tackle** you will need. Sport fishing is one of the most expensive types of fishing.

Deep sea fishing requires big fishing poles, strong line, and big hooks. The fish you are seeking to catch will determine the type of rod and tackle you will use.

It is important to have extra line, hooks, rigs, weights, and saltwater lures. You never know when a fish will snap your line.

Pliers, a filet knife, and a fish scale are other things you should have on hand. A landing net and **gaff** will be needed to help get your fish in the boat.

Deep sea fishing can be exciting, but only if you are catching fish. It is good to have both artificial and live bait on the boat.

There are many types of small bait fish that are great for your offshore fishing trip. You can buy them from a bait store or catch them with a **cast net**.

Other types of bait used for deep sea fishing include shrimp, squid, mullet, cut up fish, and ballyhoo. **Chum** is sometimes used by anglers to attract fish.

squid

FUN FACTS

Most sport fishing boats have a live well to keep your bait alive.

There are countless types of artificial bait used for deep sea fishing. **Lures**, spoons, and plugs come in all colors and sizes.

WAYS TO DEEP SEA FISH

Trolling is a common way to catch big game fish. This is when bait or lures are pulled behind the boat.

Bottom fishing is a popular way to catch grouper and snapper. Drop your line, let it sink to the bottom, and see what bites!

Another way is called deep dropping. Bait is dropped with a heavy weight 300-1500 feet (91-457 m) down in the ocean. An electric fishing reel is used for this type of fishing.

Deep drop electric reels can cost around $4,000.

Deep sea fishing is great for anglers who enjoy being on a boat. Want to try some of the most exciting fishing of your life? Get out there and find a fishing charter near you!

GLOSSARY

anchor (ANG-ker): A device usually made of metal that is attached to a boat or ship by a cable and when thrown overboard digs into the earth and holds the boat or ship in place

cast net (kast net): A net that is thrown out and then immediately drawn in again

chum (chuhm): Animal or vegetable matter thrown overboard to attract fish

deep sea fishing (deep see FISH-ing): The activity of catching fish that live in the deep parts of the sea

fishing charter (FISH-ing CHAHR-ter): A fishing boat and crew that is paid to take passengers fishing

gaff (gaf): A stick with a hook for landing large fish

lure (loor): A decoy for attracting animals to capture, especially an artificial bait used for catching fish

sailfish (SEYL-fish): A large sea fish related to the swordfish and marlin that has long slender jaws and a very large fin like a sail on the back

tackle (TAK-uhl): A set of special equipment

tuna (TOO-nuh): A large sea fish related to the mackerel often caught for food or sport

INDEX

WEBSITES TO VISIT

www.takemefishing.org/saltwater-fishing/types-of-saltwater-fishing/deep-sea-fishing/

www.mocomi.com/deep-sea-fishing/

https://pursuingoutdoors.com/deep-sea-fishing-tips-for-beginners/

ABOUT THE AUTHOR

Kerri Mazzarella was raised on the East coast of Southern Florida. She has enjoyed fishing most of her life. Her family spends the weekends on their boat deep sea fishing. All four of her teenage children are experienced anglers. Fresh fish is often on the dinner menu at their house! Kerri's favorite saltwater fish to eat is tuna.

Photographs: Shutterstock; Cover: © Al McGlashan, ©MicroOne, ©Zerbor, ©GreyMoth; Pg 3, 4,8, 12, 16, 20, 24 © ESB professional; Pg 1, 3, 8, 18, 22 © MicroOne; Pg 7, 9, 11, 13, 15, 16, 22 ©Zerbor; Pg 4 ©Go2dim; Pg 6 ©Grzegorz Lukacijewski; Pg 7 ©lidialongobardi77; Pg 8 ©lunamarina; Pg 9 ©kelldallfall, ©lunamarina; Pg 10 ©J nel, © Jason Richeux; Pg 12 ©Scharfsinn; Pg 13 ©UfaBizPhoto; Pg 14 ©MPH Photos; Pg 16 ©George P. Choma; Pg 17 ©richard pross; Pg 18 ©DUSAN ZIDAR; Pg 19 ©corners74; Pg 20 ©James Kirkikis; Pg 21 ©Susi Nodding; Pg 22 ©PitchBlack; Pg 23 ©Go2dim; Pg 24 ©lunamarina; Pg 27 ©Fabien Monteil, ©Alessandro Sarasso; Pg 28 ©Somprasong Khrueaphan

CRABTREE
Publishing Company

Written by: Kerri Mazzarella
Designed by: Kathy Walsh
Proofreader: Crystal Sikkens

Library and Archives Canada Cataloguing in Publication
CIP available at Library and Archives Canada

Library of Congress Cataloging-in-Publication Data
CIP available at Library of Congress

Crabtree Publishing Company
www.crabtreebooks.com   1-800-387-7650

Printed in the USA/072022/CG20220201

Published in the United States Crabtree Publishing
347 Fifth Avenue, Suite 1402-145
New York, NY, 10016

Published in Canada Crabtree Publishing
616 Welland Ave.
St. Catharines, Ontario L2M 5V6